D1444780

Vegetables in a Pot

Vegetables in a Pot

by D.J. Herda

*illustrated with drawings by Kathy Fritz McBride
and photographs*

Julian Messner New York

Library of Congress Cataloging in Publication Data

Herda, D. J.
    Vegetables in a pot.

    Includes index.
    SUMMARY: Offers instructions for cultivating
certain vegetables indoors in a variety of containers
such as milk cartons, old shoes, and garbage cans.
    1. Vegetable gardening—Juvenile literature.
2. Container gardening—Juvenile literature.
3. Indoor gardening—Juvenile literature.
[1. Container gardening.   2. Vegetable gardening—
3. Indoor gardening.   4.   Gardening]
I. Title.
SB324.4.H47   635'.04'8   78-23936
ISBN 0-671–32929-4

Messner books by D.J. Herda

Vegetables in a Pot

Making a Native Plant Terrarium

Vegetables in a Pot

CONTENTS

1.
Indoors or Out?

A tiny seed is placed in a hole in the soil. It is covered, patted, and watered. Within days, it has sprouted. Within weeks, it has grown.

That's an amazing process — the growth of a plant from a tiny seed. It's even more amazing when you realize it's a vegetable plant — a plant whose leaves, roots, or fruits are edible. You can eat it. It's more amazing, still, when you realize you grew it in a pot!

Most people think vegetables must be grown in a large garden or on a farm. But many vegetables can be grown in a pot. The pot may be kept indoors or outdoors when the weather is warm enough. As long as the plant receives plenty of natural sunshine and proper care, it will grow as well as it would in the ground — maybe better.

You can grow vegetables in a pot even if you live in an apartment in the city. You can grow them on a terrace or a balcony. Or you can find some space for a pot on a sunny windowsill.

The best thing about growing vegetables in a pot is that you can enjoy fresh-picked produce any time of year, whether you live in warm, sunny Florida or coldest Alaska. You can have fresh green beans and ripe red tomatoes in December, and lettuce and peppers all year round. Even strawberries grow big and juicy indoors. And, when picked fresh, they taste far sweeter and juicier than any you buy at the supermarket or take from a can.

Growing vegetables in a pot is no more difficult than growing them in the ground. Just follow a few simple instructions, find a suitable growing container, and the rest will be easy, and fun! And you'll be enjoying your own harvest of vegetables in as little as a month.

These delicious looking tomatoes are growing from a hanging pot.

Wayne checks out a cabbage plant in a pot.

2.
How Vegetables Grow

Think about it for a moment. A tomato seed lies in an envelope for years. When you remove it and examine it, it's still no more than a seed.

Yet, when you press it into the soil and water it, it sprouts into a tender, young plant.

What happens in the soil to turn a small, brown seed into a large, green plant?

Vegetable seeds are covered by a thin coating — a hard, shell-like cover. That cover keeps the embryo, the life inside the seed, from drying out and dying.

When the seed is moistened, the protective outer shell softens and splits open. The moisture reaches the embryo and tells it that it's time to begin growth, or *germination*.

The seed sends out a main root covered with tiny root hairs. Then more and larger roots begin to appear. Finally, a shoot or stalk emerges and pushes up through the soil, reaching for the sun.

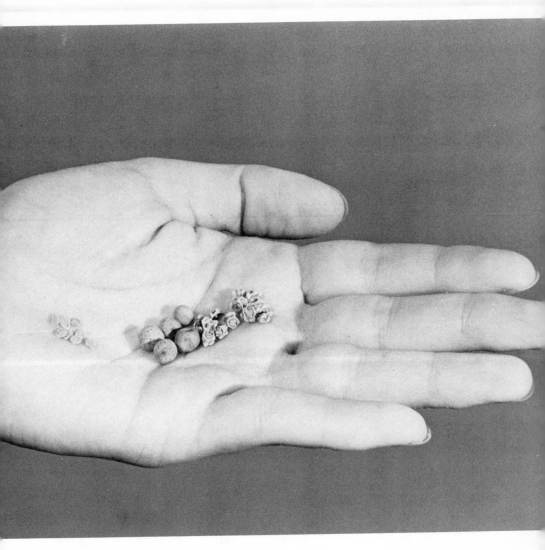

Three different kinds of seeds.

Until that stage, the seed needs only moisture for growth. However, as the stalk emerges, the roots will need moisture and nourishment, or food, which comes from tiny elements in the soil — elements far too small to see.

As the stalk continues to grow, it needs sunlight to produce healthy, green leaves. Through a process known as photosynthesis, the leaves turn sunlight into food, which the plant will use to grow.

If any of the elements of light, water, and soil are missing when the plant needs them, the plant will begin to weaken and bend. Soon, it will die.

But if the plant's needs are met, it will continue to grow larger and stronger. Some plants will produce small buds, which will turn into flowers. These flowers will finally become the fruit.

The fruit will be small at first, but gradually it will grow larger and riper. Soon, it will be ready for picking.

Some vegetable plants do not flower to produce edible fruit. Instead, they produce underground roots, which can be eaten. These plants, like radishes and carrots, are called root vegetables.

Other plants, like lettuce and spinach, produce tender, green leaves that we eat.

No matter how a plant produces, the important thing to remember is that, given its basic needs, it will bear tasty vegetables for us to enjoy.

A young, growing plant.

Wayne examines the root of his carrot plant — sweet, ready-to-eat midget carrot.

Leaf lettuce — ready for cutting and eating. New leaves will replace those cut off.

3.
Selecting the Container

The place to begin growing vegetables in a pot is with the pot. You can't plant the seed until you have a container to hold the soil.

Not all vegetables require the same size container. It should be large enough to hold the plant at maturity — when the plant is fully grown and producing.

While all seeds can be started in a pot no larger than a cup, most plants would quickly outgrow such a small container. So it's better to start the seeds off in the proper size pot from the beginning. Or else ask at your plant store for peat pots, specially made for starting plants. Then the peat pots can be planted in larger containers after the plants have sprouted.

Luckily, you don't *have* to go out and buy pots for your plants. Manufactured pots — especially the larger ones — can be expensive.

**Look around the house for discards
you can use as containers.**

If you look around the house, you'll probably find a suitable container in which to grow your vegetables. The following chart should give you an idea of the size of different household containers.

	Quart	½ Gallon	Gallon	10 Gallons
Milk Carton	•	•	•	
1-pound Coffee Can	•			
2-pound Coffee Can		•		
Ice Cream Carton	•	•		
Bleach Container			•	
Garbage Can				•

In addition to these containers, you can turn more unusual items into vegetable pots.

A large old shoe (one that nobody wants anymore!) makes an interesting container for small plants. Though a shoe isn't deep enough for root crops such as carrots or beets, it would be fine for leaf lettuce, strawberry, red pepper, and many types of low-growing herbs. The shoe could be made waterproof by filling a plastic bag with soil, then stuffing the bag inside the shoe, with the opening of the bag at the shoe's opening.

And, speaking of plastic bags, any waterproof bag can make an inexpensive container. Sizes vary from small sandwich bags to giant trash-can liners (30 gallons). The bag can be filled with soil, tied shut with a "twist-em,"

Patty certainly found an unusual planter!

and punched at the top where the seeds will be inserted. A few drainage holes should be punched at the bottom so excess water doesn't collect in the soil and drown the plants. These plastic bag planters should then be set on a tray for the excess water to run into.

An old coffee pot makes an interesting container for small vegetables. If the pot is 8 inches or deeper, it will even hold short root crops. But because a pot is only a few inches in diameter, you can't put in too many seeds. So, don't overcrowd.

A kitchen utensil that makes an excellent vegetable pot is a colander or strainer. Lined with sphagnum moss (available at most garden centers) to prevent the soil from washing out the holes, it can be used to grow strawberries, lettuce, endive, radishes — any small growing plants.

Other effective pots include plastic trash cans, shoe boxes, juice pitchers, wooden crates, and — of course — regular flowerpots. Of the commercial or store-bought pots, the ones made of clay are the best. Clay pots hold soil and moisture in while allowing air to pass through, thus preventing the soil from becoming too wet. (Saturated soil may drown the plants.) A saucer underneath the pot will collect water runoff.

One type of container you should *not* use is glass. Drilling a hole for drainage and air is too difficult. Expert growers and experienced indoor gardeners can use glass pots, because they can tell just how much to water — and how much is *too* much.

If the containers have no drainage holes, some can usually be drilled or punched in with an awl, a sharp tool used for making holes in soft material. Usually, one ½-inch drainage hole is enough for a pot 10 inches in diameter.

Containers larger than 10 inches in diameter should have three or four ½-inch holes, with the exception of clay pots, which require only one because they are *porous,* allowing air to pass through.

4.
Selecting the Seeds

Seeds are available by mail and from garden and nursery stores, as well as from many grocery, variety, and hardware stores. Often, you can find two or more varieties of nearly every commonly grown vegetable. However, if you plan on growing more unusual vegetables, small fruit trees, or special varieties, you'll probably have to order from a mail-order house. Their catalogs are free. A list of mail-order houses appears on pages 89 and 90.

Keep in mind when ordering or buying seeds to grow in pots that you have limited space. Don't plan on growing large, vining plants like pumpkins or melons, for example. And such tall plants as corn and amaranth aren't very practical for container growth.

Patty is enjoying her seed catalogs.

On the other hand, many varieties of vegetables have been developed recently for growth in pots. These are usually small, compact plants that need little soil and space to produce fruit. The best way to tell which plants are available is to order several mail-order catalogs and look through them carefully.

In the catalogs you'll find different varieties, or types, of vegetables — like Superstar, Big Boy, and Sweet 100 tomatoes — grouped together. Read the listing for each variety before deciding which to plant.

Pay particular attention to *maturity date* (the approximate time between *germination,* or when the plant pops up above the soil, and *harvest,* or when you may expect to pick the produce). Maturity dates are usually listed as a number of days. For example, under a listing for Big Boy tomato, the maturity date given is 78 days. Another variety called Burgess Early Salad Tomato matures in only 45 days — almost half the time.

Unless you're very patient, you'll probably want to select varieties of vegetables that mature quickly.

Another thing to look for when choosing a variety of vegetables to grow in pots is its *resistance to disease.* Plants with good resistance to disease are less likely to get sick and die.

If you grow your vegetables in pots indoors, using only sterilized soil, it's not likely that you'll have too many problems with disease. Still, some diseases are spread by organisms so small they can't be seen except under a microscope. These organisms may reach your plants from fresh air when you open the windows or doors of your home. Disease-resistant plants will be able to fight off these organisms and remain healthy.

Another important thing to look for when selecting seeds for growing in pots is the plant's *habit* — the way it grows. Some bean plants, for example, have vining habits that allow them to grow to 20 feet in length or longer. That makes them far too large for growing in most pots.

Other bean varieties, though, have bush habits. They form short, thick, bush-like plants just a few inches tall. These bush beans make excellent choices for pot growth.

A list of many different fruits and vegetables which grow well in pots is included in a later chapter.

Wayne, Jerry and Wade check out a vining tomato plant.

5.
Preparing the Soil

The type of soil you grow your vegetables in is important. Don't use hard, rocky soil lacking the minerals and other elements necessary for good, healthy growth. Instead, select a soil that's rich, black, and *loamy* — spongy feeling.

If you know of a place where you can dig up some good, rich soil, take a shovel and a can or a large box. Make sure you have any necessary permission. Dig up more than you think you'll need. It will always seem to be used up sooner than you predict. Then smooth out the soil so no one will trip because of the hole.

Before planting the seeds in the soil, be sure the soil is sterilized. If you dig it up yourself, place the soil in a metal pan (a disposable baking tin costs less than a dollar

Wade, Wayne, and Jerry dig up a good garden soil to use in their containers.

and can be used over and over again). Then pre-heat the oven to 350°F. (You may need adult help with this.) When the oven is ready, place the soil in the pan on the oven rack and bake it for 45 minutes.

The pan of soil will be very hot when it comes out of the oven. Don't touch it for a few hours. After the soil has cooled, all fungus and disease spores will be dead. If you don't sterilize the soil, tender young sprouts may be killed by a disease called "damping off." The seeds come up and are then attacked by a fuzzy-looking disease. Soon, the plants shrivel and die.

If you can't find enough garden soil to fill your pots or if you don't want to go through the trouble of sterilizing soil from outdoors, you can buy potting soil in many grocery, hardware, and variety stores, as well as at plant stores and nursery centers. Be sure the bag says the soil has been sterilized. That means you can safely plant the seeds in it without worrying about the young shoots being attacked by damping off and other diseases.

In order to "stretch" the soil — to make it go further — buy a small bag of sphagnum moss and a bag of vermiculite. Add one handful of each for every two handfuls of soil, either dug-up or bought.

Besides making the soil go further, the moss and vermiculite will help keep the soil nice and loose, or loamy, allowing the roots to grow easily and oxygen to circulate through the soil. The result will be healthy, hardy plants.

Soil heavily mixed with vermiculite.

6.
Preparing the Container

Once you've gathered or bought the soil for planting, you can begin getting the container ready. The first thing to do is make sure the container is clean. Wash plastic and clay pots or metal cans in warm, soapy water, and rinse clean. Wooden containers may be soaked in hot water (the utility room or basement sink is a good place) and then removed and allowed to dry.

Next, add some drainage material to the container. This will help keep the soil at the bottom of the pot from becoming too wet. Cover the drainage holes with a piece of screening, fiberglass, or nylon stocking to prevent the drainage material from falling out. After that, add 1 to 3 inches of small pebbles, aquarium gravel, or other coarse material to the bottom of the container. Add more for deep containers, less for shallow ones.

Finally, fill the container to within 2 inches of the top with sterilized soil. Firm the soil down with your hand, add more, and firm again to within 2 inches of the top.

At this point, you're ready to begin planting.

7.
Planting the Seeds

It's never easy to know how many seeds to plant in a single pot. Most seed packages give advice on how closely to plant seeds outdoors in the garden — but not in a small container.

As you gain more experience in container gardening, you'll know how large a pot you'll need for a single tomato plant, or how many radish plants you can fit into a 6-inch pot. Until then, you can use the following method to give you a rough estimate.

When planting small seeds like carrots and lettuce, plant more than the larger seeds, like beans and peas. The plants that sprout from the smaller seeds are delicate. Many will die before they have a chance to grow. If you plant many small seeds, you'll be sure to get at least some that will grow into healthy, young plants.

How many is enough? For very small seeds (lettuce, carrots, cabbage), plant two seeds to every inch of container space measured across the top. For medium-sized seeds (beets, tomato), plant one seed to every inch of container space. For large seeds (beans, peas), plant one seed to every 2 inches of container space.

Small seeds should be planted by carefully placing them on top of the soil in the container. Then cover the seeds with soil about twice the depth of the seed itself. For the tiniest seeds, just a light sprinkling of soil — barely enough to cover them — is enough.

Larger seeds should be planted by making a hole in the soil twice as deep as the size of the seed, inserting the seed, and covering it with soil.

After the seeds have been covered, press the soil down firmly with your hand. Squeeze out any pockets of air in the soil which might dry out the seeds before they have a chance to grow. Water the soil lightly. Don't drench it!

Next, place a sheet of plastic wrap across the top of the container, without touching the soil. The plastic will keep the moisture and heat in. You shouldn't have to water again until after the seeds have sprouted.

If, after a few days, the soil seems too moist or if you see fungus, a gray mold, beginning to form on the top of the soil, you have over-watered. While there's no way you can remove excess water from the soil, you *can* remove the plastic covering for a day or two until the soil dries out a bit.

A tiny seed being planted near the surface of the soil.

Firming up. . . .

Gentle spraying. . . .

And a cover of plastic wrap.

From the time you plant the seeds until they've sprouted, keep the container in a warm but not hot location — out of direct sunlight. Seeds don't need sunlight until they've developed their second set of leaves. If you place the seeds or tiny plantlets in direct sun, they may be scalded and die before they ever have a chance to grow.

When the seeds are warm and moist, they begin to germinate, or sprout. The length of time you'll have to wait for germination depends on the seed. Usually, thick-skinned seeds, like beans and peas, require a longer time to germinate. Thin-skinned seeds like radishes and to-matoes require less time. The backs of the seed packages should tell you how long you'll have to wait to see those first tiny shoots appear above ground.

As a seed pokes its head above ground, the first thing you'll see is a thin white loop as the stem of the plant begins to lift out of the soil. This is the time you should remove the plastic cover from the container.

Check the soil as the young plants emerge. If it feels dry when you stick your finger into it, you should water lightly with a fine-sprinkling can or a clothes sprayer. Don't pour heavy streams of water onto the plants or you may knock them over or uproot them.

Usually, within a day or two, the first set of leaves will appear on the plant. These are not true leaves but are called "heart leaves." They will be followed within a couple more days by "true leaves," which are thicker and look more like the plant's permanent leaves.

True leaves.

This second set of leaves means the plants are now seedlings, and they can be gradually moved to direct sunlight to grow. Give them two hours of sunlight the first day, five or six the second, and a full day's worth after that. This will harden off the plants — get them used to the high heat of the sun a little at a time.

The next part of the growing process is always the most difficult. You will probably have a potful of young, healthy-looking seedlings before you. Now you must thin out — remove some of them — so that the remaining plants will receive enough light, water, food, and root space to grow well and produce. If the pot is over-crowded with seedlings, all the plants will grow poorly and will probably set little or no fruit.

With a pair of small scissors (manicure scissors work well), snip off the smallest, least healthy-looking plants, until only one plant remains for each 3 to 6 inches of soil.

It's difficult to say *exactly* how many plants to let grow in the pot, since small plants require less growing room than large ones. Experience is the best way to judge, but until you gain that experience, here's a guideline you can follow.

If, after the plants are several weeks old, they grow so large that their leaves begin to touch one another or the plants appear to be crowded, thin out the least healthy-looking plants. Your plants will need plenty of growing space — even if it means thinning back to only one plant

Ouch! — But it's necessary.

per container. After all, it's better to have one healthy, bearing plant than ten small, scrawny plants that never develop fruit.

Remember when thinning plants to cut them at the soil line with a pair of scissors — never pull them out. By pulling out plants from a crowded pot, you could disturb the roots of the remaining plants. That would cause the growth of the remaining plants to slow down or stop.

8.
Water, Light, Temperature, Humidity

These four elements are necessary for plants to grow healthy and strong. All plants — whether grown indoors or out, in pots or in the ground — require them. But they require only the proper amount, not too much and not too little.

Water

How much water you give your plants is every bit as important as when you water them. With too little water, the plants will dry up and die. With too much water, they will become saturated. The roots will begin to rot and the plants will die.

How do you know the right amount of water to give your plants? The best way to tell is by using the "finger test."

Every other day, press your finger into the soil up to the first knuckle. If you remove your finger and it's covered with wet, sticky soil, the plant needs no watering. If your finger comes out clean, however, the plant needs water.

Water only enough so that the excess begins to flow out the drainage hole on the bottom. (Put the pot in the sink or in a tray or saucer to catch the excess water so it doesn't ruin the carpet, floor, or table.)

Wait about 15 minutes and check the plant again. If there's water sitting in the saucer, empty it. Never leave a container sitting in a puddle of water or you'll damage the plant's root system.

Many indoor gardeners prefer to use water that has been sitting in a gallon jug, pitcher, or watering can overnight. While that's not necessary (unless there's a lot of chlorine in your water — ask your parents), it's important to use water that isn't too cold or too hot. It should be comfortably cool — about room temperature (60-70°F). Hot water may damage the roots and scald the stem of the plant. Very cold water may shock the plant and stop its growth.

Light

We've already discussed the importance of light for producing good, healthy plants. Flowering plants, both fruit and vegetables, need up to 16 hours of light each day. That means you should keep the pots near a window

The finger test for watering.

Wade waters a blossoming pepper plant.

that faces south or west to gather as much sunlight as possible. If that can't be done or when the days are short, ask your parents to set up a grow-light fixture for your plants.

A grow-light is a special type of light that contains all the same rays as natural sunlight. Regular house light bulbs do not.

To grow your plants under a grow-light, check the directions that come with the bulb. The plants should not be too close to the bulb or they may burn. If they're too far from the light, the plant will have weak, scraggly stems that won't flower or bear fruit.

Most plants grown under grow-lights should be placed about 5 to 8 inches away from the bulb, depending on the bulb's strength. A little experimenting will show you the best distance at which the plants thrive.

Patty is surely doing all the right things by the looks of these vegetables in pots!

Temperature

Growing plants in a room that is too hot is just as bad as growing them in a room that is too cold. Vegetables need temperatures that are about the same as the outdoor temperatures at which they grow best.

Some plants, like lettuce, peas, and spinach, grow well in cool temperatures — from 50-70°F. Often, you can change the temperature where your plants are growing by placing them nearer to or farther from a window.

In the winter, when windows are cold, lettuce, peas, and spinach will grow best near the glass. In the summer, when windows heat up, they'll do best set back several inches. The opposite is true with beans, radishes, tomatoes, and other warm-weather plants.

Humidity

Humidity is a measurement of the moisture, or water, in the air. All plants need a certain amount of humidity. Without it, their leaves will become dry and brittle.

Humidity is rarely a problem during summer months. There's usually plenty of moisture in the air, unless you live in a hot, dry climate like Southern California or Arizona.

However, low humidity *is* a problem during winter months. There's rarely enough moisture in the air to satisfy plants.

Spraying vegetables in pots helps them stay fresh and
healthy on hot summer days. Spraying should be done early
in the morning before it gets too hot so the water won't
evaporate too quickly.

You can raise the humidity around your plants by setting the containers in a tray that has been lined with small pebbles or sphagnum moss. Keep the bottom of the tray moist (but don't allow pots to sit in a pool of water). The moisture in the tray will slowly evaporate and float up around the plants' leaves. This will keep the leaves soft and green and the plants growing well, no matter how dry the rest of the house is.

Another way to treat plants to extra humidity is to buy a fine spray bottle or plant-mister and spray around the plants daily.

9.
Food for Thought

All plants need food. While seeds will germinate without food, young plants will soon begin to droop and finally die without a well-balanced diet.

Some pre-packaged, commercial soils have good food already added. It's generally just enough to get young seedlings off to a good start. But as your potted plants grow larger and require more nutrients, you'll have to feed them.

The main elements in a plant's diet are nitrogen, phosphorous, and potassium (also called potash). In general, plants use nitrogen to produce good, green foliage. Phosphorous is used to produce healthy flowers and fruit. Potassium helps roots grow healthy and well.

Nitrogen is needed most by leafy vegetables like lettuce, spinach and chard. Phosphorous is needed by flowering vegetables like tomatoes and peppers. Potassium is needed by root vegetables like carrots, radishes, and beets.

Jerry adds a commercial plant food to the sprinkling can.
It's important to follow the directions carefully or the
plant may be damaged.

Of course, other elements are important for healthy plant growth, too. Trace elements — meaning those available only in small amounts — play an important role in a plant's healthy growth. So it's best to use a plant food that contains not only the three main elements, but a good selection of trace elements, as well.

When you buy a plant food, or fertilizer, you'll see three numbers listed on the label in this manner: 5-10-5, 7-7-14, or something similar. These three numbers refer to the percentage of the three main elements included in that plant food. The elements are listed in alphabetical order (first nitrogen, then phosphorous, and finally potassium).

So, if you want a food high in nitrogen for leaf vegetables, buy a plant food that contains the highest percentage of nitrogen (like 10-5-5). For a food rich in phosphorous, 5-10-5 would be best. A potassium-rich food would be 5-5-10 or something similar.

Of course, if you buy a plant food for each different type of vegetable you grow, you could spend quite a lot of money. One food may be best for tomatoes, another for carrots, a third for lettuce, and so on. Rather than that, consider buying just one all-purpose food whose phosphorous percentage is about twice as high as its nitrogen and potassium. That means a food like 5-10-5, 3-6-3, 7-14-7, and so forth.

Besides differing in the three main elements, plant foods vary in form. Some come as liquids, some as tablets, some as granules to be sprinkled on top of the soil, and others as powders to be dissolved in water before use. The form makes no difference to the plants. Buy something that's easiest to use.

When should you fertilize your plants? There are three especially good times.

First, 3 to 4 weeks after the seedlings have sprouted. Then, just before the plants produce fruit. Finally, midway through the fruiting season (or, in the case of non-flowering leaf and root vegetables, about midway through their growth season).

But be careful! Follow the instructions on the plant food bottle or box and don't overfeed! Overfeeding potted plants can do more harm than good. Too much nitrogen, especially, will cause roots and leaves to burn, which may kill the plants.

Remember: when in doubt, it's better *not* to feed than to overfeed. If you follow directions closely, you should have no problems. Your plants should grow healthy, strong, and fast.

10.
Suggested Varieties for Growing in Pots

The following is a list of fruit and vegetable varieties that have grown well in pots. The time listing (28 days, etc.) refers to the length of time between sprouting and harvesting. The time may vary, though, under different growing conditions.

This list is only a general guide for you to follow in choosing plants to grow in pots. If you find something you'd like to grow that's not on this list, go ahead and try it. That's the only way you'll ever know whether or not it will work.

The suggested pot size following each listing is a minimum. Larger pots may be used.

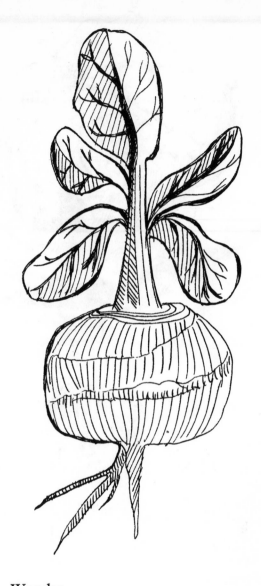

BEETS, Early Wonder
52 days
Smooth-skinned, globe-shaped fruits grow to 3 in. across.
Allow 6-10 in. across and 6 in. deep for each plant.

CABBAGE, Golden Acre
64 days
This plant produces firm, small heads of good eating quality, reaching 7 in. Allow 8-10 in. across and 8 in. deep for each plant.

CABBAGE, Dwarf Modern
55 days
These tiny 4-in. heads are firm and round, with a very sweet taste. Allow 8 in. across and 6-8 in. deep.

CANTALOUPE, Minnesota Midget
60 days
This remarkable plant produces midget, 4-in. fruits that
are very sweet and edible to the rind. The plants grow
on a 3-ft. vine. Allow 8-10 in. across and 8 in. deep.

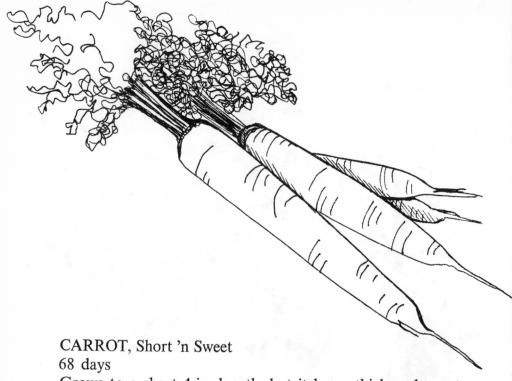

CARROT, Short 'n Sweet
68 days
Grows to a short 4-in. length, but it has a thick and sweet root. The fern-like tops are attractive as houseplants. Allow 4-5 in. across and 6 in. deep.

CARROT, Little Finger
65 days
One of the smallest carrots, this reaches a length of only 3 in. Allow 3 in. across and 5 in. deep.

CARROT, Tiny Sweet
62 days
Midget 3-in. carrots are crisp and sweet! Good for even heavy hard soils. Allow 3 in. across and 5 in. deep.

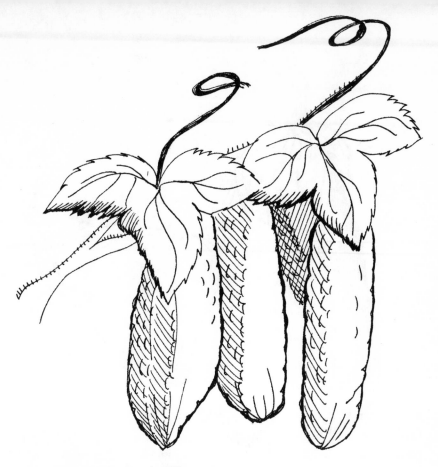

CUCUMBER, Bush Whopper

55 days

Whopping big cucumbers, 6-8 in. long, are produced on
this short, non-vining plant. Excellent in salads. Fruit must
be shielded by leaves from direct sun to prevent scalding.
Allow 8-10 in. across and 10 in. deep.

CUCUMBER, Patio Pik

51 days

A compact, dwarf vining plant with fruit that grows from
4-6 in. long. Allow 6-10 in. across and 8 in. deep.

71

EGGPLANT, Mission Bell Hybrid
70 days
Deep purple fruits are produced on strong, firm stems reaching 2 ft. in height. Allow 12 in. across and 10-12 in. deep.

EGGPLANT, Modern Midget
65 days
Earliest of all eggplants are produced on small, bushy plants. Allow 6-8 in. across and 8-10 in. deep.

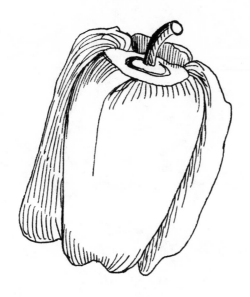

GREEN PEPPER, Park's Whopper Hybrid
65 days
These huge fruits are produced on compact, disease-resistant plants. If left to mature beyond 65 days, the green
fruits will turn a deep red and have a sweet taste. Allow
8-10 in. across and 8 in. deep.

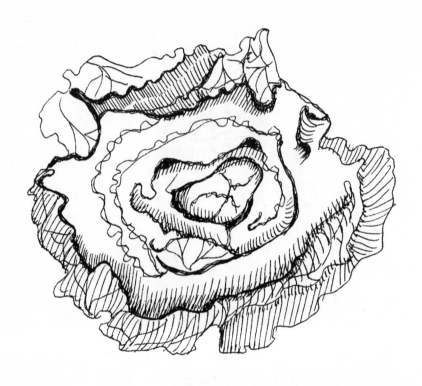

HEAD LETTUCE, Tom Thumb
65 days
These tennis-ball-sized heads are crisp and sweet and make excellent salad servings as picked. Allow 6 in. across and 6 in. deep.

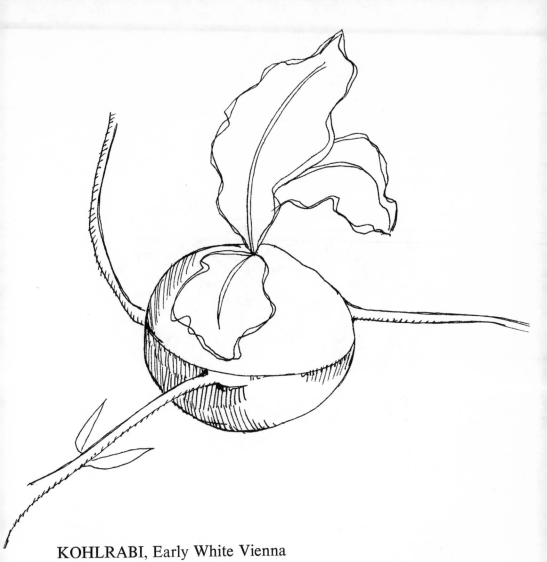

KOHLRABI, Early White Vienna
55 days
Excellent, sweet white fruit which may be peeled and
eaten raw or cooked. Allow 5-8 in. across and 6 in. deep.

LEAF LETTUCE, Oak Leaf
40 days
This fast-growing lettuce is crisp and tasty in salads. Allow
1 in. across and 4 in. deep. (Unlike most plants, leaf lettuce *can* be crowded and grows well when plants' leaves
are touching.)

ONION, Evergreen White Bunching
120 days
These silvery-white long onions grow in clusters of from
4-9. Allow 2 in. across and 8-10 in. deep.

PEAS, Mighty Midget
60 days
These tiny, 3-in. pods are produced on vines only 6-in.
long. Allow 4 in. across and 6 in. deep.

POLE BEAN, Selma Star
60 days
A new pole bean introduced this year by Park produces
many dark green beans on vines which wander to 6-ft.
Train on a trellis or on the hangers of a hanging basket.
Allow 8 in. across and 8-10 in. deep.

POMEGRANATE, Dwarf Ornamental
time varies
Bright, orange-red flowers are followed by unusual red
fruits. A good pot plant. Allow at least a 10 gal. container
for a mature plant.

RADISH, White Icicle
28 days
This novel, long white radish has a rich, spicy taste, growing to 5 in. Allow 3 in. across and 7-10 in. deep.

RADISH, Champion
28 days
Bright, cherry-red fruits are most tender and mild if pulled
when small. Allow 3 in. across and 6-8 in. deep.

SPINACH, America

28 days

Glossy, deep-green leaves are attractive and make good eating fresh or cooked. Allow 3 in. across and 6 in. deep.

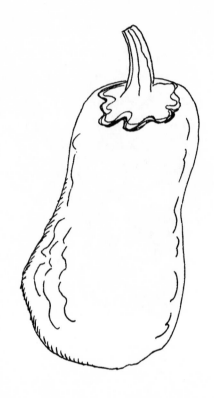

SQUASH, Creamy Hybrid
55 days
This attractive, dwarf plant spreads to 18 in. and produces
white fruits from 6-8 in. in length. Allow 12-18 in. across
and 12 in. deep.

STRAWBERRY, Alexandria (Best grown from plants)
time varies
A plant that produces no runners, this yields pretty white
flowers followed by firm, sweet, red berries. Plants grow to
10 in. Allow 8-10 in. across and 8 in. deep.

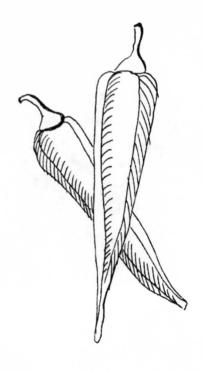

SWEET PEPPER, Sweet Banana
65 days
This heavy-producing pepper has fruits that turn sweet
and red at maturity. Allow 6-8 in. across and 8 in. deep.

TOMATO, Sweet 100 Hybrid
65 days
Attractive, disease-resistant plant produces many small salad-sized fruits on a plant that may hang or be staked. Allow 8-10 in. across and 8 in. deep.

TOMATO, Better Boy VFN Hybrid
70 days
This plant produces a great many full-sized fruits while resisting common tomato diseases. Stake firmly for support. Allow 10-12 in. across and 10 in. deep.

TOMATO, Bitsy VF Hybrid
62 days
An excellent miniature tomato for container growing, producing medium-sized fruits ideal in salads. Allow 8-10 in. across and 8 in. deep.

The following is a list of seed companies that offer mail-order service and free catalogs.

Burgess Seed & Plant Co.
Galesburg, Mich. 49053

Burpee Seed Co.
Warminster, Penn. 18991

Farmer Seed & Nursery Co.
Faribault, Minn. 55021

Henry Field Seed & Nursery Co.
Shenandoah, Iowa 51602

Gurney Seed & Nursery Co., Inc.
Yankton, S. Dak. 57078

Kelly Bros. Nurseries
Dansville, N.Y. 14437

J. W. Jung Seed Co.
Randolph, Wis. 53956

L. L. Olds Seed Co.
Madison, Wis. 53701

Geo. W. Park Seed Co., Inc.
Greenwood, S.C. 29647

R. H. Shumway Seeds
Rockford, Ill. 61101

Stark Bros. Nurseries
Louisiana, Mo. 63353

Index

plant diseases, 33
plant food. *See* food.
planting seeds, 41-42
plants, number of per pot, 49-51
pole bean, 79
pomegranate, 80
pot; size of, 19, 20, 21; manufactured
    pots, 24; kinds of pots, 24;
    cleaning, 40; wooden, 40;
    drainage, 40; number of seeds per
    pot, 41-42
potash. *See* potassium.
potassium, 61-64
pumpkin, 30

radishes, 18, 28, 41, 47, 58, 61, 81, 82
red pepper, 26
resistance to disease, 32-33
root hairs, 15
roots, 15, 16, 38
root space, 49
root vegetables, 18, 24, 65; *see also*
    carrots, radishes

sandwich bags. *See* bags.
seed, 11, 15, 19; where to get seeds,
    30-32; how many per pot, 41;
    large, 41, small, 42
seed catalog, 30, 32
seedlings, 49
Selma Star Pole bean, 79
shoe, as container, 24-26
shoe box, as container for plants, 28
shoots, 15, 47
Short'n Sweet carrot, 70
Shumway, R. H., Seeds, 90
soil, 14; rocky, 38; sterilized, 32;
    36-38; moisture content, 42, 61
soil, commercial, 61
sphagnum moss, 38
spinach, 18, 58, 83
spores, 38

sprouts, 38, 47
squash, 84
stalk, 15
Stark Brothers Nurseries, 90
sterilized soil, 32; 36-38, 40
strainer, 28
strawberry, 26, 28, 85
stretching soil, 38
sunlight, 47, 49; 57
Superstar tomato, 32
Sweet Banana Sweet pepper, 86
Sweet 100 Hybrid tomato, 87
Sweet 100 tomato, 32, 87
sweet pepper, 86

temperature, 58; of water, 53
thinning out plants, 49-51
Tiny Sweet carrot, 70
tomatoes, 14, 32, 41, 42, 47, 58, 87,
    88. *See also* named brands.
Tom Thumb Head lettuce, 74
trace elements, 64
trash can, as container for plants, 28

vegetables, grown in a pot, 13;
    harvesting, 13, 32; early maturing
    varieties, 32; and temperature,
    57-58; and light, 57; and water, 57;
    and food, 61-65; and humidity,
    58-61; varieties, 67-88
vegetable garden, 11
vegetable seeds, 15; where to get
    them, 30-32. *See also* listing, 89.
vegetable varieties, 67-88
vermiculite, 38
vining habit, 33

watering plants, 42, 47, 49;
    water, 52-53
White Icicle radish, 81
window, 58
wooden containers, 40

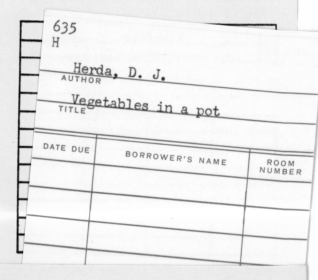

635
H

Herda, D. J.
Vegetables in a pot

635
H

Herda, D.J.
AUTHOR

Vegetables in a pot
TITLE

DATE DUE	BORROWER'S NAME	ROOM NUMBER

635
H

Herda, D.J.
    Vegetables in a pot